HASH CAKES

> " I think pot should be legal. I don't smoke it, but I like the smell of it. "
> Andy Warhol

...who's been eating my cake?

Preferred hash: blond
Hash quantity:
half baked = 4 g (^{1}/7 oz)
well baked = 6 g (^{1}/4 oz)

Preferred hash: black
Hash quantity:
half baked = 4 g ($^1/_7$ oz)
well baked = 6 g ($^1/_4$ oz)

GW00726956

HASH CAKES

HASH CAKES

HOW TO MAKE GREAT SNACKS WITH CANNABIS

DANE NOON & LEX LUCID

spruce

An Hachette UK Company
www.hachette.co.uk

First published in Great Britain in 2011 by Spruce
a division of Octopus Publishing Group Ltd
Endeavour House
189 Shaftesbury Avenue
London
WC2H 8JY
www.octopusbooks.co.uk

978-1-84601-372-0

Printed and bound in Hong Kong

10 9 8 7 6 5 4 3 2 1

Contents

Introduction

How Cannabis Works

Cannabis is a bit like the beanstalk in the famous fairy tale: it's a magical plant. Both cannabis and the beanstalk are grown from magic seeds and both will help you get high enough to talk to people who live in the clouds. There was a hidden message in the Jack and the Beanstalk fairy tale – if you don't want to get eaten by giants, stay off the Cheeba Cheeba.

But how is it that a common weed like cannabis can have such magical properties? The secret of its potency lies in an active ingredient called THC. Other chemicals called CBD and CBN join this and together they go looking for canniboid receptors around the body and brain. Once the

THC has bonded with the receptors the cannabis is working, at which point you shouldn't work, especially if you're operating heavy machinery. Cannabis affects you in exactly the same way as a naturally occurring brain chemical, which is a great argument for why you were *meant* to get stoned.

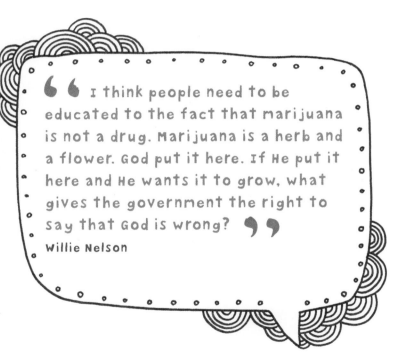

" I think people need to be educated to the fact that marijuana is not a drug. Marijuana is a herb and a flower. God put it here. If He put it here and He wants it to grow, what gives the government the right to say that God is wrong? "

Willie Nelson

The Lowdown on the Hash High

A cannabis high lasts for about two to three hours, and the most notable effects on the body are an increased heart rate, a dry mouth and tingling in the hands or feet. Psychologically, you'll perceive a sharpening of colour and sound, a rapid flow of creative (sometimes profound) ideas, and an uncontrollable giggling sensation. You will find yourself laughing at anything, no really, anything. It could be something as mundane as the hairs growing out of your partner's ear, or a cat – not even a cat in a funny hat, just a regular house cat. All in all you will feel euphoric, relaxed and stress free.

Although consuming too much cannabis can produce some unwanted side effects like dizziness, numbness and a prolonged period of sleep (I once witnessed an over eater take a seven-hour nap at the top of the stairs), these are relatively harmless. Sure, you'll probably forget what day of the week it is, or imagine yourself as a Che Guevara type fighting for the pride of your cul-de-sac against tyrannical garbage-men, but that will wear off by the following morning. In fact, in order to take a lethal dose of cannabis you would have to eat more hash than you could physically stomach, so relax.

A Unique Experience

The effects of cannabis can differ drastically from person to person depending on personal perceptions and tolerance levels. Some people enjoy cannabis on a social level, while for others it remains a completely personal activity. The relaxation experienced after consuming cannabis removes barriers and allows us to connect with people on a more personal level. On top of this, the periods of introspection might see you examining and unravelling your deep inner workings in search of the root to your soul.

Holy Men around the world have taken cannabis for thousands of years to aide meditation and soul searching, and it seems to have worked for them.

The only difference is you won't have to spend years in a bald-headed, cross-legged abstinence. Let it take you on a journey and believe me when I say: doing nothing will never be as much fun. Enjoy yourself and spread the love.

The Medicinal Properties of Cannabis

Although most cannabis users indulge for recreational highs, this majestic plant also has a number of medical applications: it truly is a miracle drug. It has been used to relieve the symptoms of multiple sclerosis, glaucoma, insomnia, weight loss, arthritis and cancer. In fact, the list goes on and it's easy to see why there has been so much campaigning behind the headlines. Several countries around the world have now legalized the use of marijuana for medical purposes, but it remains a tightly controlled drug.

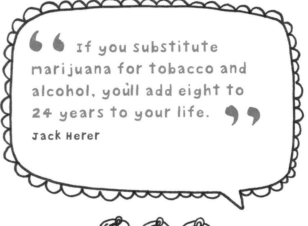

" If you substitute marijuana for tobacco and alcohol, you'll add eight to 24 years to your life. "
Jack Herer

Cannabis Strengths & Types

I wasn't drunk, it was the skunk!

Cannabis is a bit like fine wine in that it's most appreciated by connoisseurs, or potheads, as they're known. To the amateur there are just two types of marijuana and that's weed and hash. However, the stoner is well aware of the wonderful world of plants being pollinated and cross-pollinated around the world. There is weed from Jamaica, hash from Nepal and skunk from Amsterdam; then there's oil from Thailand – black hash oil and blond hash oil. There are Sativa plants that give an energetic high and Indica plants that take the floor out from under your feet.

Different plants have widely differing strengths and produce different effects, so there's a real sense of trial and error when it comes to sampling your key ingredient. You can expect anything from a calm, mellow high to euphoria that leaves you unable to function.

Opposite is a guide to some of our favourite hash varieties from around the world.

Hash variety	Grown	Characteristics	Strength
Royal Afghani	All over Afghanistan	Produced using Indica plants then hand rolled. Heavy high.	4/5
Nepali Temple Ball	Nepalese mountains	Very rare hash, originally used by temple monks.	5/5
Moroccan Standard	Foothills of Rif Mountains in Morocco	Popular variety giving clean and uplifting high.	2/5
Charas	India	Hand-rolled hash used by holy men. Strong high.	3/5
Triple Zero	Morocco	Winner of 2008 Cannabis Cup for Best Import. Contains most potent resin glands. Very strong.	5/5
Neder Hash	The Netherlands	Rare outside Holland, available in different forms. Super strong.	6/5

The Hash Files

There are two main types of hash: the soft, dark, squidgy 'black hash' made in places like Nepal, Afghanistan and India, and the lighter, harder 'blond hash', which hails from Morocco and Lebanon. Black hash is made by hand and it's labour intensive work that involves living plants being rubbed until the resin sticks on the farmer's hands and is rolled into balls. It is said that the sweatier the hands that rub your hash, the better the high. Well, that might not be strictly true, but when you're about to indulge in some Nepalese Temple Ball (one of the finer hand-rolled hashes of the world) it's nice to know that you and a Himalayan farmer are about to form a special kind of bond.

Blond hash is made by passing the dried plants through a series of increasingly fine sieves. The finest sieve sees the sticky, potent part of the plant, known as 'kief', fall. The plants are usually sieved about four times, and each step of the process produces a different grade of hash. With the exception of top grade blond hashes, most of these varieties contain more plant material and less THC than black hash.

For the recipes in this book we recommend a good hash, as it is easier to cook with. But if you can only get your hands on weed or skunk, we'll guide you through the process of making that into a tasty treat.

Variety is the Spice of Life

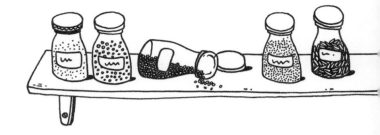

The variety of weed and skunk available for your eating pleasure has exploded in the last 35 years. Most locally available varieties will also be produced locally and the quality and strength can go up and down like a pogo stick.

As a general rule, weed will give you a mellow high whereas skunk will happily hit you for a home run. The names of the different strains are as colourful and endless as the experiences you can expect when you try them out. There's Jack Herer, White Widow, Orange Bud, Purple Haze, Silver Haze, Jamaican Gold, Thai Stick, Bubblegum, Blueberry and Cheese, to name but a few. Unless you travel to Amsterdam for your hashish hit, it's almost impossible to guarantee that you're buying the genuine article. Telltale signs of a top-notch toke are a strong, fragrant aroma and sticky buds glistening with crystals.

To help you make a well-informed choice when it comes to the more specialized part of your grocery shopping, we've provided a guide to what type of hash you'll need to add to each of our scrumptious recipes. And each recipe also tells you how much hash you'll need to use for either a half-baked or well-baked experience. Ultimately though, quantities and qualities will boil down to personal choice and whether you want to get slightly stoned or seriously baked.

The Culinary Experience

Cooking and eating cannabis is an age-old tradition in North Africa, and it was actually the preferred method of consumption for the 19th-century stoners of the West.

There are plenty of benefits to cooking, rather than smoking, cannabis. You'll cut the number of roach butts in your ashtray, get rid of the smoky haze in your house and reduce the risk of simmering spliffs burning holes in your sofa. Then there's the obvious health benefit – smoking is bad for you, even if you are toking on the sweet herb of life.

When you smoke cannabis, less than 10 per cent of the active ingredient enters your body temple. When you eat it you get 100 per cent of the magic ingredient coursing through your inner space. The effects are by no means as instantaneous. It can take an hour or even two before you feel the effects, by which time you may have lost faith in the gods of Cheeba Cheeba. Whatever you do, don't get too impatient and go for a second helping before the first has kicked in – this could wind up being mildly disastrous.

If it's your first time trying cannabis, just give it time. But even if you consider yourself a veteran 'Cheech' or 'Chong' in the smoking department, and this is your first foray into cannabis food, be warned that it will be a stronger and longer high than you're used to.

HIGH TEA!

The Subtle Stoner

Including cannabis in your cooking, or making cannabis butter and spreading it on toast (see the recipe for CannaButter on pages 22–25), is a much more discreet way of getting high than toking on a massive spliff. You may well be permanently converted to the smoke-free high. If you do choose to become a regular marijuana eater, remember to clearly label your stash and store it away from the herb cupboard in your kitchen. It might be hilarious to discover that Auntie Ethel has sprinkled it over her Bolognese, but anyone who unwittingly ingests dope can end up having a confused and scary night.

The best way to enjoy a culinary cannabis session is to organize a social gathering at your place. Sort out your supplies, fire up the oven and choose a recipe from one of the many culinary delights in this book. Surround yourself with soft lighting, comfy furnishings and a repertoire of suitable stoner music.

It goes without saying that you should get baked – especially for the first time – with people you know well, so keep the invite list to your closest friends.

Most importantly, enjoy yourself. Getting stoned can be a warm and enlightening experience that eases stress and gets your creative juices flowing: a great antidote to the hustle and bustle of everyday life.

Cooking with Cannabis

In this book you will find an array of sweet and savoury culinary masterpieces all lovingly prepared with everyone's favourite 'magic' ingredient. Our top tip for cooking with hash is simple – mix it in – thoroughly! Failure to do this will result in what is known throughout the counter-culinary industry as a game of muffin roulette. Quite simply, if you don't mix it in well, all of the hash will end up in one of the cookies while the rest will have none. You'll have an overly happy friend who quickly has to turn to bed and then sleeps over for a day or two.

To help achieve the top tip another tip is to make sure the hash is grated or crumbled as finely as you can get it. Invest in a small spice grater – it'll be invaluable in the endeavours highlighted by this book. When using soft hashes, just keep plucking and picking at the hash until it's ready. Think of this as a therapeutic activity. By making sure it's as fine as you can, it will be easier to digest and the effect more constant – no big waves of 'stonedness'.

CannaButter

You might be sat there without any hash, twitching your curtains, working up the courage to venture outside and ask the none-too-pleasant 'connect' down the street for a nice big bag of Cheeba Cheeba. Or you might have already found the heart of a lion, but also found that what that so-and-so gave you is not hash but skunk or weed instead. Fear not, here's a recipe that turns skunk into CannaButter, a somewhat un-delicious alternative to hash.

CannaButter can be lovingly added to any dish that calls for butter as an ingredient. For the recipes in this book, simply replace the normal butter with CannaButter and omit the hash from the ingredients list.

Making cannabis butter is quite simple although it takes a bit of time; and the timing is crucial. To extract maximum THC from finely ground cannabis, you simmer a cannabis–water mix for up to 24 hours. But you don't want to cook the CannaButter for any longer than 24 hours! That's right: NO MORE THAN 24 HOURS. After 24 hours the THC will degrade and the butter will go bitter. To make 350 g (12 oz) of CannaButter follow the recipe on pages 24–25.

How to make cannabutter

The ingredients

450 g (1 lb) unsalted butter, 480 ml (16 fl oz) water, 25 g (1 oz) premium, middle or low-grade cannabis. (Obviously the better product you use the more potent the butter will be.)

The method

Begin by grinding the cannabis material to a fine powder using a strong grinder.

Pour 480 ml (16 fl oz) of water into a heavy-based saucepan and bring to a steady boil over a medium-high heat. Once boiling, add your butter and melt it in the water. Reduce the heat to very low, then whisk in the cannabis until thoroughly combined, there are no clumps and nothing is stuck to the bottom of the saucepan. Place on the lid and leave to cook at a VERY gentle simmer for 22–24 hours. Remember, NO MORE THAN 24 HOURS! During this cooking period you will need to check on the butter mixture every few hours to ensure that the simmer is not too strong and the butter has not reduced too much. If you find the solution reducing faster than expected, add a few tablespoons of water. This won't ruin your finished product.

Once you've simmered the butter mixture for long enough, turn off the heat and let sit for 2–4 minutes. Meanwhile, place a large square of

also good on toast

cheesecloth over a bowl. Make sure it is big enough that it won't disappear with the liquid when you pour it into the bowl. Pour the butter mixture and strain off the bits of cannabis. Once you've strained all the mixture and the cannabis material is collected in the cheesecloth, carefully squeeze the cheesecloth to extract as much of the butter solution as you can. This is what you want; not the soggy cannabis bi-product.

Place the bowl of butter solution in your refrigerator and let cool for a few hours, even overnight. This process will separate the fats from the water. Let sit long enough to ensure the complete separation of the fats from the water.

Removing the butter from the bowl may seem a bit tricky...but will be considerably less messy if you use heavy-duty cling film to handle the now solid butter. Use the cling film to remove the top slab of CannaButter from the bowl and then pat it dry with kitchen towel to remove any excess water.

Now use more cling film to compress the CannaButter into smaller, more manageable portions. Store the little packets in an airtight container in the freezer. If kept in the freezer, the CannaButter won't lose any potency before you get around to using it.

Happy churning!

The Spiritual Home of the Stoner

Although smoking weed outside the privacy of your own home is still frowned upon in most places, tokers can take refuge in the coffee shops of Amsterdam.

This city became a stoner's paradise in 1976 when they decided to turn a blind eye to the type of criminal found giggling and clutching a small bag of Cheeba Cheeba. Registered shops in Amsterdam (cafés) offer a selection of different weeds and hashes so you can get high to your heart's content. Some of the world's strongest strains of cannabis have originated in the cultivation houses of Holland. However, although a trip to Amsterdam can be enlightening, remember that ordering a 'strong black' in a café will more likely land you with a big bag of hash than a caffeine-based drink.

The good thing about being in a café is that snacks are generally on hand. Smoking marijuana gives you cravings known as the munchies. Chocolate cake, cheesecake, walnuts, stale pizza and soft leather boots are often eaten in excessive quantities. When eating hash cakes, this can present a 'catch 22' situation where eating one cake will necessitate the eating of them all, often with disastrous consequences. So, always make sure you have a good spread of munchies to hand when you embark on an evening of pot taking.

A SLICE OF
HEAVEN

History, Facts & Trivia

Sitting around consuming cannabis can result in lengthy periods of reflection, hilarity and downright nonsense. It's therefore no great surprise that there are endless facts and stories relating to this potent plant. For starters, what do you call it? Marijuana has enough names to rival a phone book and these include Cannabis, Pot, Ganja, Skunk, Hash, Cheeba Cheeba and sweet Mary-Jane.

The long list of titles is hardly surprising when you consider that the first recorded use of cannabis was in 6000BC – there's certainly been plenty of time to come up with new names for the holy herb. It also means plenty of time for production techniques to evolve.

A Bumper crop

It seems hard to believe that before 1937, Hemp was one of the most widely grown crops in the world. It was used for fuel, papermaking, clothes, rope, and, of course, getting high. There was even a law stating that farmers had to grow the now illegal plant. George Washington once said, 'make the most of hemp, sow it everywhere.' So, why is it illegal? Despite the talk by right-wing politicians that cannabis is dangerous, this actually had nothing to do with its demise as a commercial crop. The powers that be decided that hemp threatened the profits of the cotton, fossil fuel and plastic industries, so it was banished to the naughty step.

Famous Tokers

Cannabis might have been officially obliterated, but people around the world had come to appreciate the finer qualities of the plant and they weren't going to be put off by anything so trivial as laws. Today, a staggering 22 million people smoke weed daily. This is the same number of people who have been jailed for marijuana related offences in America since its prohibition in 1937. That's 22 million people behind bars in a country where the Declaration of Independence was written on Hemp paper. The cannabis advocates include celebrities, past and present. It's estimated that during his lifetime Bob Marley smoked enough pot to fill an articulated lorry! Abraham Lincoln was once quoted as saying, 'Two of my favourite things are sitting on my front porch smoking a pipe of sweet hemp, and playing my Hohner harmonica.' That's right, the 16th President of the United States was a pothead.

" When I was a kid I inhaled ... frequently ... that was the point. "
Barack Obama

Space Cakes

Blondies

Preferred hash: blond
Hash quantity:
half baked = 4 g (^{1}/7 oz)
well baked = 6 g (^{1}/4 oz)

500 g (1 lb) white chocolate,
    roughly chopped
75 g (2^1/$_2$ oz) butter
3 eggs
180 g (6^1/$_2$ oz) cup caster sugar
180 g (6^1/$_2$ oz) self-raising flour
180 g (6^1/$_2$ oz) macadamia nuts,
    roughly chopped
Hash
1 teaspoon vanilla extract

Makes 18

1. Preheat the oven to 190°C/375°F/Gas Mark 5. Grease a 26 x 18 x 2.5-cm (11 x 7 x 1-inch) baking tin and line the base with greaseproof paper.

2. Set aside 400 g (14 oz) of the white chocolate. Melt the remaining chocolate and butter in a small bowl set over a saucepan of simmering water. Cool slightly.

3. Beat the eggs and sugar together in a bowl and gradually beat in the melted chocolate. Sift the flour over the mixture and then fold in together with the chopped macadamia nuts, reserved chocolate, finely crumbled hash and vanilla extract.

4. Pour the mixture into the prepared pan and bake for 25–30 minutes until the centre is only just firm to the touch. Let cool for 10 minutes before cutting into squares. Lift the blondies out carefully with a palette knife. Serve slightly warm or cool completely and store in an airtight container between layers of greaseproof paper.

Blueberry & Vanilla Muffins

175 g (6 oz) unsalted butter, melted
Hash
150 g (5 oz) ground almonds
150 g (5 oz) caster sugar
50 g (2 oz) self-raising flour
4 egg whites, lightly beaten
1 teaspoon vanilla extract
150 g (5 oz) blueberries

Makes 10

1. Preheat the oven to 190°C/375°F/Gas Mark 5. Line 10 sections of a muffin tray with paper cases.

2. Melt the butter slowly over a gentle heat. Crumble the hash into the melted butter and stir continuously until it dissolves. Make sure the butter does not bubble or split. Keep stirring.

3. Mix together the ground almonds, sugar, flour and hash butter. Add the egg whites and vanilla extract and mix until smooth. Spoon the batter into the paper cases and scatter with the blueberries.

4. Bake in the preheated oven for 15 minutes until just firm in the centre. Let cool for 5 minutes and then transfer the cupcakes to a wire rack to cool.

one of your
five a day!

The Ultimate Chocolate Brownie

Preferred hash: black
Hash quantity:
half baked = 4 g (^{1}/7 oz)
well baked = 6 g (^{1}/4 oz)

200 g (7 oz) dark chocolate, broken
    into chunks
200 g (7 oz) butter
3 eggs
1 teaspoon vanilla extract
1 tablespoon strong espresso (or
    1 tablespoon coffee granules
    dissolved in 1 tablespoon hot water)
1 cup caster sugar
100 g (3^3/4 oz) plain flour
^{1}/4 teaspoon salt
Hash
75 g (2^1/2 oz) walnuts, roughly chopped
75 g (2^1/2 oz) pecan nuts, roughly
    chopped

Makes 12–16

1. Preheat the oven to 180°C/350°F/Gas Mark 4. Grease a 34 x 20 x 2.5-cm (13 x 9 x 1-inch) baking tin and line the base with greaseproof paper.

2. Melt the chocolate and butter together in a small bowl set over a saucepan of simmering water. Let cool for 5 minutes.

3. Beat the eggs in a bowl with the vanilla extract, espresso and sugar until well combined, then beat in the melted chocolate mix. Add the flour and salt and beat until smooth. Crumble the hash into the mixture – it can be in chunky bits if you want. Stir in with the roughly chopped nuts. Pour the brownie mixture into the prepared baking tin.

4. Bake in the preheated oven for 25–30 minutes. Be careful not to overcook; the sides should be firm but the centre still slightly soft. Let cool for 10 minutes before cutting into squares. Lift the brownies out carefully with a palette knife. Serve slightly warm with double cream, or cool completely and store in an airtight container between layers of greaseproof paper.

Jamaican Rum Cake

Hash
625 g (1¼ lb) mixed dried fruit
100 g (3½ oz) glacé cherries, halved
250 ml (8 fl oz) dark rum
2 tablespoons black treacle
175 g (6 oz) unsalted butter, softened
175 g (6 oz) dark muscovado sugar
4 eggs, beaten
200 g (7 oz) self-raising flour
2 tablespoons ground ginger

Makes 12–16 slices

only one cup
of rum?

1. Put the hash, mixed dried fruit, glacé cherries and dark rum in a large bowl. Give the mixture a good stir, cover and leave for 24 hours, stirring occasionally.

2. Preheat the oven to 150°C/300°F/Gas Mark 2. Grease an 20-cm (8-inch) round cake tin and line the base with greaseproof paper.

3. Drain 400 g (14 oz) of the fruit from the bowl using a slotted spoon and purée in a food processor with the black treacle.

4. Beat together the butter and sugar until creamy. Gradually beat in the eggs, a little at a time, adding a little of the flour if the mixture starts to curdle. Using a large metal spoon, stir in the remaining flour, ground ginger, fruit and rum mixture, including any unabsorbed rum, and the fruit purée. Continue to stir until well combined. Pour the mixture into the prepared baking tin and level the surface.

5. Bake in a preheated oven for 2½–3 hours until firm or until a skewer inserted into the centre comes out clean. Let cool in the tin.

Chocolate Fudge Cake

Preferred hash: black
Hash quantity:
half baked = 4 g ($^1/_7$ oz)
well baked = 6 g ($^1/_4$ oz)

100 g (3$^1/_2$ oz) unsweetened cocoa
  powder
100 g (3$^1/_2$ oz) plain dark chocolate,
  finely chopped
200 g (7 oz) unsalted butter, softened
325 g (11 oz) light brown sugar
275 g (9 oz) self-raising flour
$^1/_2$ teaspoon baking powder
3 eggs, beaten
Hash

Fudge icing
300 g (10 oz) plain dark chocolate,
  broken into chunks
200 g (7 oz) unsalted butter, softened
225 g (7$^1/_2$ oz) icing sugar

Makes 12 slices

1. Preheat the oven to 180°C/350°F/Gas Mark 4. Grease two 20-cm (8-inch) round cake tins and line with greaseproof paper.

2. Whisk the cocoa powder in a bowl with 300 ml (½ pint) boiling water until smooth. Stir in the chopped chocolate and let cool, stirring occasionally.

3. Beat together the butter, sugar, flour, baking powder and eggs until smooth. Add the hash and chocolate mixture and beat until combined. Divide the batter evenly between the tins and level the surface.

4. Bake in the preheated oven for 20–25 minutes or until just firm to the touch. Transfer to a wire rack to cool.

5. To make the frosting, melt the chocolate in a small bowl set over a pan of simmering water. Remove from the heat and let cool slightly. Beat the butter and icing sugar together until creamy, then beat in the melted chocolate until smooth. Sandwich the cakes together with some icing, then pile the remainder on top, spreading it evenly over the top and sides.

Carrot & Nut Traybake

Preferred hash: black or blond
Hash quantity:
half baked = 4 g (^{1}/7 oz)
well baked = 6 g (^{1}/4 oz)

300 g (10 oz) self-raising flour
350 g (12 oz) caster sugar
2 teaspoons baking powder
100 g (3^1/2 oz) Brazil nuts, chopped
2 teaspoons ground cinnamon
1 teaspoon ground ginger
300 ml (^{1}/4 pint) vegetable oil
300 g (10 oz) carrots, grated
4 eggs, beaten
1 teaspoon vanilla extract
Hash

For the topping
400 g (14 oz) low-fat cream cheese
1 tablespoon honey
Brazil nuts, chopped, to decorate

Makes 18 slices

1. Preheat the oven to 180°C/350°F/Gas Mark 4. Grease a 30 x 23 x 5-cm (12 x 9 x 2-inch) baking tin and line the base with greaseproof paper.

2. Put the flour, sugar, baking powder, Brazil nuts, ground cinnamon and ground ginger in a large bowl. Add the oil, grated carrots, eggs, vanilla extract and hash and beat together until well combined. Pour the batter evenly into the prepared tin.

3. Bake in the preheated oven for about 50 minutes or until firm to the touch. Let cool in the pan for 5–10 minutes, then turn out on to a wire rack to cool completely.

4. For the topping, combine the cream cheese and honey in a bowl. Spread the mixture evenly over the top of the cake and decorate with the chopped Brazil nuts. Serve in slices or squares.

OM NOM NOM!

Gingerbread

Preferred hash: blond
Hash quantity:
half baked = 6 g ($^1/_4$ oz)
well baked = 8.5 g ($^1/_3$ oz)

500 g (1 lb) self-raising flour
1 tablespoon ground ginger
$^1/_2$ teaspoon bicarbonate of soda
$^1/_2$ teaspoon salt
Generous $^3/_4$ cup light brown sugar
175 g (6 oz) unsalted butter
175 ml (6 fl oz) black treacle
175 ml (6 fl oz) golden syrup
Hash
300 ml ($^1/_2$ pint) milk
1 egg, lightly beaten

Makes 24 slices

1. Preheat the oven to 180°C/350°F/Gas Mark 4. Grease a 30 x 20-cm (12 x 8-inch) cake tin and line the based with greaseproof paper.

2. Sift the flour, ground ginger, baking soda and salt into a bowl. Put the sugar, butter, black treacle and golden syrup into a saucepan and heat gently until the butter has melted and the sugar has dissolved.

3. Pour the liquid into the dry ingredients together with the hash, milk and egg, then beat with a wooden spoon until smooth. Pour the mixture into the prepared tin.

4. Bake in the preheated oven for 1$^1/_4$ hours or until a skewer inserted into the centre comes out clean. Let cool in the pan for 10 minutes and then turn out on to a wire rack to cool. Wrap the cooled cake in aluminium foil to store.

Fruit Tea Loaf

Preferred hash: black
Hash quantity:
half baked = 3.5 g (^{1}/8 oz)
well baked = 6 g (^{1}/4 oz)

Hash
300 g (10 oz) mixed dried fruit, such as sultanas, currants, raisins and glacé cherries
125 g (4 oz) light brown sugar
125 g (4 oz) unsalted butter
200 ml (7 fl oz) brewed tea
2 teaspoons ground allspice
Finely grated rind of 1 orange
225 g (7^1/2 oz) self-raising flour, sifted
1 tablespoon honey, warmed

Makes 8–10 slices

a magic mixture of fruit, honey and hash!

I. Place the hash, mixed dried fruit, sugar, butter, brewed tea and ground allspice in a saucepan. Cover and heat gently until the butter has melted, stirring occasionally. Bring to a boil and boil for 1 minute, then remove the pan from the heat. Add the orange rind. Set aside and leave overnight.

2. Preheat the oven to 180°C/350°F/Gas Mark 4. Grease a 450-ml (15^3/4 fl-oz) loaf tin and line the base with greaseproof paper.

3. Fold the sifted flour into the fruit mixture until well combined. Spoon the mixture into the prepared tin and level the surface.

4. Bake in the preheated oven for 50–55 minutes or until golden and a skewer inserted into the centre comes out clean. Remove the cake from the oven, brush the top of the cake with warmed honey and let cool completely in the tin. Turn out and serve in slices spread with butter, if liked.

Vanilla Cupcakes

Preferred hash: blond
Hash quantity:
half baked = 4 g (^{1}/7 oz)
well baked = 6 g (^{1}/4 oz)

150 g (5 oz) lightly salted butter, softened
150 g (5 oz) caster sugar
175 g (6 oz) self-raising flour
3 eggs
1 teaspoon vanilla extract
Hash

For the buttercream
150 g (5 oz) unsalted butter, softened
250 g (8 oz) icing sugar, sifted
1 teaspoon vanilla extract
2 teaspoons hot water

Makes 12

1. Preheat the oven to 180°C/350°F/Gas Mark 4. Line a 12-section, standard-size muffin tray with paper cases.

2. Put all the cake ingredients and hash in a large bowl, then beat with a hand-held electric whisk until light and creamy. Divide the cake batter between the cupcake cups.

3. Bake in the preheated oven for 20 minutes or until risen and just firm to the touch. Transfer the cupcakes to a wire rack to cool.

4. To make the buttercream, put the butter and icing sugar in a bowl and beat well until creamy. Add the vanilla extract and hot water and beat again until smooth. Spread over the cooled cupcakes. Alternatively, put the mixture in a piping bag fitted with a star nozzle and pipe swirls of buttercream on the tops.

...best served with a nice cup of tea

Rock Buns

Preferred hash: blond
Hash quantity:
half baked = 6 g (^{1}/4 oz)
well baked = 8.5 g (^{1}/3 oz)

125 g (4 oz) unsalted butter, softened
100 g (3^1/₂ oz) caster sugar
Hash
225 g (7^1/₂ oz) self-raising flour
1 teaspoon each ground ginger and
    cinnamon
1 egg, beaten
150 ml (^{1}/₄ pint) milk
100 g (3^1/₂ oz) sultanas
75 g (3 oz) currants
50 g (2 oz) white sugar cubes

Makes 20

1. Preheat the oven to 190°C/375°F/Gas Mark 5. Grease two baking sheets.

2. Cream together the butter and sugar until light and fluffy. Stir in the hash, flour, ground ginger and cinnamon, egg and milk, then mix to a soft dough. Stir the sultanas and currants into the mixture. Place spoonfuls of the dough onto the baking sheets, spacing them slightly apart.

3. Put the sugar cubes in a freezer bag and lightly crush with a rolling pin. Scatter the sugar over the buns and bake in the preheated oven for about 15 minutes or until risen and golden. Transfer the buns to a wire rack to cool.

just like mother made!

Lemon & Poppy Seed Cake

175 g (6 oz) butter, softened
175 g (6 oz) caster sugar
3 eggs, beaten
250 g (8 oz) self-raising flour
Hash
1 teaspoon baking powder
40 g (1$^1/_2$ oz) poppy seeds
Grated rind and juice of 2 lemons

To finish
125 g (4 oz) icing sugar
3–4 teaspoons lemon juice

Makes 10 slices

1. Preheat the oven to 160°C/315°F/Gas Mark 2–3. Grease a 22 x 12 x 6-cm (8$^1/_2$ x 4$^1/_2$ x 2$^1/_2$-inch) loaf tin and line with greaseproof paper.

2. Beat the butter and sugar together in a mixing bowl until pale and creamy. Gradually mix in alternate spoonfuls of beaten egg and flour until all has been added and the batter is smooth. Stir in the hash, baking powder, poppy seeds, lemon rind and 5–6 tablespoons lemon juice to make a soft dropping consistency. Pour the batter into the prepared loaf tin and spread the surface level.

3. Bake in the preheated oven for about 1 hour or until well risen, the top is cracked and golden and a skewer inserted into the centre comes out clean.

4. Let cool in the tin for 10 minutes, then loosen the edges and lift out of the pan using the greaseproof paper. Transfer to a wire rack, peel off the paper and let cool. To finish, sift the icing sugar into a bowl, then gradually mix in enough of the lemon juice to make a smooth coating glaze. Drizzle over the top of the cooled cake.

Tea & Bliss-cuits

Chocolate Chip Cookies

Preferred hash: black
Hash quantity:
half baked = 4 g (^{1}/7 oz)
well baked = 6 g (^{1}/4 oz)

125 g (4 oz) unsalted butter, softened
50 g (2 oz) caster sugar
50 g (2 oz) vanilla-flavoured sugar
1 egg
150 g (5 oz) rolled oats
Hash
150 g (5 oz) self-raising flour
250 g (8 oz) milk chocolate, roughly
    chopped

Makes 18–20

1. Preheat the oven to 180°C/350°F/Gas Mark 4. Lightly grease two large baking sheets.

2. Put the butter and sugars in a mixing bowl and beat together until pale and creamy. Beat in the egg, then add the rolled oats, hash and flour and stir until combined. Stir in the chocolate.

3. Place heaped spoonfuls of the cookie dough on the greased baking sheets, spacing them well apart. Flatten the dough pieces slightly with the tines of a fork.

4. Bake in the preheated oven for 15–20 minutes or until they are risen and pale golden. Let firm up on the baking sheets for 5 minutes and then transfer to a wire rack to cool completely.

...full of oaty goodness!

48

Peanut Butter Cookies

125 g (4 oz) unsalted butter, softened
150 g (5 oz) light brown sugar
125 g (4 oz) chunky peanut butter
Hash
1 egg, lightly beaten
150 g (5 oz) plain flour
^{1}/2 teaspoon baking powder
125 g (4 oz) unsalted peanuts

Makes 28

1. Preheat the oven to 180°C/350°F/Gas Mark 4. Lightly grease three large baking sheets.

2. Put the butter and sugar in a mixing bowl and beat together until pale and creamy. Add the peanut butter, hash, egg, flour and baking powder and mix together until combined. Stir in the peanuts.

3. Take large teaspoonfuls of dough and position onto the baking sheets, leaving a good 5-cm (2-inch) gap between them to allow for spreading. Flatten slightly.

4. Bake in the preheated oven for 12 minutes or until golden around the edges. Let cool slightly on the baking sheets for a few minutes and then transfer to a wire rack to cool completely.

what's not to like?

Oats & Raisin Cookies

Preferred hash: black
Hash quantity:
half baked = 4 g (^{1}/7 oz)
well baked = 6 g (^{1}/4 oz)

Hash
150 g (5 oz) plain flour
150 g (5 oz) rolled oats
1 teaspoon ground ginger
^{1}/2 teaspoon baking powder
^{1}/2 teaspoon bicarbonate soda
150 g (5 oz) light brown sugar
50 g (2 oz) raisins
1 egg, lightly beaten
125 ml (4^1/2 fl oz) vegetable oil
4 tablespoons milk

Makes 10–12

1. Preheat the oven to 200°C/400°F/Gas Mark 6. Lightly grease a baking sheet.

2. Mix together the hash, flour, rolled oats, ground ginger, baking powder, bicarbonate soda, sugar and raisins in a large bowl.

3. In another bowl, mix together the egg, vegetable oil and milk. Make a well in the centre of the dry ingredients and pour in the egg mixture. Mix together well to make a soft dough.

4. Place heaped spoonfuls of the cookie dough on the greased baking sheets, spacing them well apart. Flatten the dough pieces slightly with the tines of a fork.

5. Bake for about 10 minutes or until golden. Let cool slightly on the baking sheets for a few minutes and then transfer the cookies to a wire rack to cool completely.

Melting Moments

Preferred hash: blond
Hash quantity:
half baked = 4 g ($^1/_7$ oz)
well baked = 6 g ($^1/_4$ oz)

175 g (6 oz) butter, softened
50 g (1$^3/_4$ oz) caster sugar
1 egg yolk
Hash
175 g (6 oz) plain flour
Grated rind of $^1/_2$ orange or lemon
1 tablespoon orange or lemon juice
Mixed peel, for decoration
Icing sugar, for dusting

Makes 20

1. Preheat the oven to 190°C/375°F/Gas Mark 5. Lightly grease two baking sheets.

2. Cream the butter and sugar together until light and creamy, then beat in the egg yolk. Mix in the hash, flour and orange or lemon rind and juice to form a smooth, thick paste.

3. Spoon the paste into a piping bag fitted with a large star nozzle, and pipe rosettes measuring about 5 cm (2 inches) across on to the baking sheets. Lightly press a little mixed peel into each cookie.

4. Bake in the preheated oven for 15–20 minutes or until pale golden. Let cool on the baking sheets for a few minutes and then transfer to a wire rack to cool completely. Dust each cookie with icing sugar.

...don't eat them
all at once

Mother's Flapjacks

Preferred hash: black
Hash quantity:
half baked = 4 g ($^1/_7$ oz)
well baked = 6 g ($^1/_4$ oz)

Hash
100 g (3$^1/_2$ oz) margarine
100 g (3$^1/_2$ oz) white vegetable fat
100 g (3$^1/_2$ oz) demerara sugar
4 tablespoons golden syrup
350 g (12 oz) rolled oats

Makes 16 slices

These flapjacks
are far out!

1. Preheat the oven to 180°C/350°F/Gas Mark 4. Grease a 33 x 23 x 5-cm (13 x 9 x 2-inch) baking tin and line the base with greaseproof paper.

2. Put the hash, margarine, vegetable fat, sugar and golden syrup in a medium saucepan. Stir over a low heat until the margarine and fat are melted and the sugar has dissolved. Remove from the heat and stir in the rolled oats until evenly coated.

3. Transfer the mixture to the prepared baking tin and spread it out, gently pressing it down so the surface is even.

4. Bake in the preheated oven for 35 minutes or until the mixture is deep golden all over. Remove from the oven and immediately score into 16 slices. Let cool in the tin and then cut into slices.

Almond Macaroons

Preferred hash: blond
Hash quantity:
half baked = 4 g (^{1}/$_7$ oz)
well baked = 6 g (^{1}/$_4$ oz)

2 egg whites
100 g (3^1/$_2$ oz) caster sugar
Hash
125 g (4 oz) ground almonds
Blanched almonds, to decorate

Makes about 20

Tip

If you would prefer not to pipe the mixture (not the smoking pipes but the cooking type), simply drop spoonfuls onto the baking sheet. These classic, chewy favourites can be served as they are or decorated with 'scribbles' of melted plain chocolate.

1. Preheat the oven to 180°C/350°F/Gas Mark 4. Line a large baking sheet with greaseproof paper.

2. Whisk the egg whites until stiff. Gradually whisk in the sugar, adding a spoonful at a time, until the mixture is thick and glossy. Fold in the hash and ground almonds. Try to be delicate with the mixture – the more air in the mixture the better.

3. Spoon the mixture into a large freezer bag, squeezing it gently into a corner. Snip off the corner of the bag and pipe small rounds, about 4 cm (1^1/$_2$ inches) in diameter, onto the baking sheet spacing them slightly apart. Press a blanched almond into the top of each one.

4. Bake in the preheated oven for 15–20 minutes until only just firm. Leave on the baking sheet to cool.

GO NUTS!

Masala Chai

6 teaspoons Darjeeling tea leaves
1 cup milk
$^1/_4$ teaspoon ground ginger
$^1/_4$ teaspoon crushed cardamom seeds
$^1/_8$ teaspoon ground cloves
1 cinnamon stick
1 tablespoon sugar
1 litre (4 cups) water
Hash

Serves 4

1. Put all the ingredients into a large saucepan over a medium heat and bring to a rolling boil. Reduce the heat to low and simmer for 5–6 minutes.

2. Strain into four large mugs or glasses. Serve hot.

...shall I be mother?

Mexican Hot Chocolate

Preferred hash: black
Hash quantity:
half baked = 0.5 g (^{1}/56 oz)
well baked = 1 g (^{1}/28 oz)

500 ml (2 cups) full-fat milk
50 g (2 oz) ground almonds
45 g (1¹/₂ oz) caster sugar
2 teaspoons ground cinnamon
1 vanilla pod, split down the centre
100 g (4 oz) plain dark chocolate,
    broken into chunks
Hash

Serves 2

1. Place the milk, ground almonds, sugar, cinnamon and vanilla pod in a medium saucepan and bring to a boil over a low heat. Take off the heat and let infuse for 20 minutes.

2. Pour the mixture through a very fine sieve into a clean saucepan, squeezing out the milk from the ground almonds.

3. Add the chocolate and hash and stir over a low heat until the chocolate has melted. Serve immediately.

hee hee!

Pot Party Food

Vanilla Ice Cream

Preferred hash: blond
Hash quantity:
half baked = 1.5 g ($^1/_{16}$ oz)
well baked = 1.75 g ($^1/_{14}$ oz)

300 ml ($^1/_2$ pint) single cream
1 vanilla pod
Hash
4 egg yolks
50 g (2 oz) caster sugar
300 ml ($^1/_2$ pint) double cream

To serve
Your favourite topping and sprinkles

Serves 6

...just add sprinkles

1. Put the single cream in a heavy-based saucepan. Split the vanilla pod, scrape out the seeds and put the seeds, pod and hash in with the cream. Place the saucepan over a low heat and bring to just below boiling point. Remove from the heat and let infuse, then remove the vanilla pod.

2. Meanwhile, put the egg yolks and sugar in a heatproof bowl and set over a pan of simmering water. Stir until thick and creamy. Gradually stir in the vanilla cream mixture. Continue stirring for 15 minutes, or until the custard coats the back of the spoon. Remove from the heat and let cool.

3. Pour the vanilla mixture into a freezer container, cover and freeze for about 45 minutes. Whip the double cream until it just holds its shape. Remove the vanilla mixture from the freezer, beat thoroughly and then fold in the whipped cream. Return the mixture to the freezer container, cover and freeze for a further 45 minutes. Beat again until smooth. Freeze the ice cream for at least a further 1$^1/_2$–2 hours before serving with your favourite topping and sprinkles.

Simple Chocolate Fudge

Preferred hash: black
Hash quantity:
half baked = 1.5 g ($^1/16$ oz)
well baked = 1.75 g ($^1/14$ oz)

60 g (2 oz) unsalted butter
120 g (4 oz) plain dark chocolate,
  broken into chunks
Hash
360 g (12 oz) icing sugar, sifted

Makes about 25 squares

1. Line the base of an 20-cm (8-inch) square baking tin with greaseproof paper.

2. Melt the chocolate and butter together in a small bowl set over a saucepan of simmering water. Add the hash. Let cool for a couple of minutes, then stir until smooth.

3. Beat half the icing sugar into the melted chocolate mix, then stir in a tablespoon of boiling water. Repeat with the remaining icing sugar and a further tablespoon of boiling water.

4. Spoon the fudge into the prepared pan, level the surface and refrigerate until hard. Cut into small squares.

...easy peasy

Golden Nugget Popcorn

Preferred hash: blond
Hash quantity:
half baked = 1 g (^{1}/28 oz)
well baked = 1.75 g (^{1}/14 oz)

1 tablespoon vegetable oil
75 g (3 oz) popcorn kernels
5 tablespoons golden syrup
25 g (1 oz) butter
Hash
50 g (2 oz) roasted cashews,
　roughly chopped

Makes about 6 cups

1. Heat the oil in a large, heavy-based saucepan with a tight-fitting lid over a medium heat for about 1 minute. Add the popcorn kernels, cover with the lid, and shake gently to coat the kernels in oil. Cook until the popping sound stops, shaking occasionally.

2. Pour the popcorn into a large bowl and set aside while you make the golden syrup coating.

3. Heat the golden syrup in a small saucepan with the butter until melted, then stir in the hash and chopped cashews. Cool slightly then pour over the popcorn and toss until the popcorn is evenly coated. Put the popcorn in a serving bowl and start munching.

party time!

Dark Chocolate Fondue

Preferred hash: blond
Hash quantity:
half baked = 1 g (^{1}/28 oz)
well baked = 1.75 g (^{1}/14 oz)

250 g (8 oz) plain dark chocolate,
  finely chopped
Hash
15 g (^{1}/2 oz) unsalted butter
2 tablespoons double cream
40 g (1^{1}/2 oz) gracé stem ginger,
  chopped finely

To serve
Fresh strawberries
Grapes
Marshmallows
Fudge or soft caramels

Serves 4

1. Melt the chocolate with the hash, butter, cream and glacé ginger in a medium-sized bowl set over a saucepan of gently simmering water, stirring occasionally.

2. Once the chocolate and butter have melted and the ingredients are well combined, remove the saucepan from the heat, empty out the water and dry thoroughly. Carefully pour the chocolate fondue into the dried saucepan.

3. Serve immediately with fresh strawberries, grapes, marshmallows and soft caramels or fudge, for dunking.

switch off the TV...
it's fondue time!

Tahini Hummus

Preferred hash: blond
Hash quantity:
half baked = 1.5 g (^{1}/16 oz)
well baked = 1.75 g (^{1}/14 oz)

Hash
400 g (14 oz) tin chickpeas, rinsed
    and drained
2 tablespoons tahini
3 garlic cloves, chopped
125 ml (4 fl oz) lemon juice
Pinch of ground cumin
Vegetable stock or water (optional)
Paprika or chopped flat-leaf parsley,
    to garnish

To serve (optional)
Carrot sticks
Celery sticks
Pita bread

Serves 6

1. Place the hash, chickpeas, tahini, garlic, lemon juice and ground cumin in a food processor or blender. Process until smooth, adding a little vegetable stock or water if you prefer a thinner consistency. Taste and add more garlic, lemon juice or cumin, if liked.

2. Transfer the hummus to a serving bowl and sprinkle with paprika or chopped parsley. Serve with carrot sticks, celery sticks and pita bread, or simply use as an alternative to spread on bread.

get dipping!

Spiced & Salted Nuts

Preferred hash: blond
Hash quantity:
half baked = 1 g (^{1}/28 oz)
well baked = 1.75 g (^{1}/14 oz)

15 g (^{1}/₂ oz) butter
1 tablespoon light olive oil
400 g (14 oz) whole mixed nuts
1 tablespoon ground paprika
^{1}/₂ teaspoon cayenne
2 teaspoons cumin seeds, lightly
 crushed
Hash
Sea salt flakes, for sprinkling

Makes 3 cups

1. Melt the butter with the oil in a frying pan. Add the mixed nuts and spices.

2. Gently fry the mixture, stirring continuously, until the nuts are lightly coloured.

3. Remove from the heat and cool slightly. Use a slotted spoon to strain off any excess butter mix and transfer to a bowl. Season with finely crumbled hash and salt flakes. Store in an airtight container for up to one week.

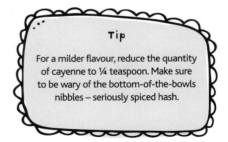

Tip

For a milder flavour, reduce the quantity of cayenne to ¼ teaspoon. Make sure to be wary of the bottom-of-the-bowls nibbles – seriously spiced hash.

Main Meals & Munchies

Spicy Lentil & Tomato Soup

1 tablespoon vegetable oil
1 large onion, finely chopped
2 garlic cloves, finely chopped
1 small green chilli, deseeded and finely
    chopped
1 cup red lentils, washed and drained
1 bay leaf
3 celery sticks, thinly sliced
3 carrots, thinly sliced
1 leek, thinly sliced
1.5 litres (2½ pints) vegetable stock
Hash
400 g (14 oz) tin chopped tomatoes
2 tablespoons tomato paste
½ teaspoon each ground turmeric and
    ginger
1 tablespoon chopped coriander leaves
Pepper

Serves 4

1. Heat the oil in a large saucepan, add the onion, garlic and chilli and fry gently for 4–5 minutes until softened.

2. Add the lentils, bay leaf, celery, carrots, leek and stock. Cover the pan and bring to a boil, then reduce the heat and simmer for 30–40 minutes until the lentils are soft. Remove the bay leaf.

3. Stir in the hash, chopped tomatoes, tomato paste, ground turmeric and ginger and coriander leaves, then season with pepper. Allow the soup to cool a little and then transfer to a liquidizer or food processor. Blend until smooth, adding more stock or water if necessary. Reheat the soup gently.

4. Pour the soup into warmed bowls and serve immediately.

Irish Stew

Preferred hash: black
Hash quantity:
half baked = 1.5 g ($^1/_{16}$ oz)
well baked = 1.75 g ($^1/_{14}$ oz)

750 g (1³/₄ lbs) boned lamb shoulder
1 tablespoon plain flour
2 tablespoons vegetable oil
3 onions, cut into wedges
400 g (14 oz) carrots, cut into chunks
875 g (2 lbs) potatoes, scrubbed and
    quartered
Hash
900 ml (1¹/₂ pints) chicken or lamb
    stock
2 bay leaves
Several sprigs fresh thyme
2 tablespoons Worcestershire sauce
Salt and pepper

Serves 4–5

I. Preheat the oven to 180°C/ 350°F/Gas Mark 4. Cut the lamb into 2.5-cm (1-inch) cubes, discarding any excess fat. Season the flour with salt and pepper and coat the lamb.

2. Heat the oil in a large frying pan. Add the lamb and fry for 5–8 minutes until lightly browned. Remove the lamb with a slotted spoon and transfer to a large flameproof casserole dish. Add the onions and carrots to the frying pan and fry until lightly browned. Put into the casserole dish along with the potatoes.

3. Add the hash, stock, bay leaves, thyme and Worcestershire sauce to the frying pan and bring to a boil. Pour the lamb mix into the casserole dish, season lightly with salt and pepper, then cover and cook in the preheated oven for 1 hour. Remove from the oven and let cool. Chill in the refrigerator for up to 24 hours.

4. To serve, place the casserole dish over a medium heat and bring the stew almost to a boil. Reduce the heat, cover with a lid and simmer gently for 25 minutes or until very hot.

Chilli Con Carne

Preferred hash: black
Hash quantity:
half baked = 1 g ($^1/28$ oz)
well baked = 1.75 g ($^1/14$ oz)

1 tablespoon vegetable oil
1 red onion, finely chopped
1 garlic clove, finely chopped
250 g (8 oz) extra-lean minced beef
Hash
1 small red pepper, cored, deseeded
    and diced
400g (14 oz) tin chopped tomatoes
1 tablespoon tomato paste
2 teaspoons chilli powder
200 ml (7 fl oz) beef stock
400 g (14 oz) tin red kidney beans,
    drained and rinsed
Salt and pepper
Cooked brown rice, to serve

Serves 2

1. Heat the oil in a heavy-based, nonstick saucepan over a medium heat. Add the onion and garlic and cook for 5 minutes or until beginning to soften. Add the minced beef and cook for a further 5–6 minutes or until browned all over.

2. Stir in the hash, red pepper, chopped tomatoes, tomato paste, chilli powder and stock. Bring to a boil, then reduce the heat and simmer gently for 30 minutes.

3. Add the red kidney beans and cook for a further 5 minutes. Season to taste with salt and pepper and serve with the brown rice.

Tortilla Wraps with Refried Beans

Preferred hash: blond
Hash quantity:
half baked = 0.5 g (^{1}/56 oz)
well baked = 1 g (^{1}/28 oz)

250 g (8 oz) tin refried beans
2 tablespoons chilli sauce
2 red peppers, cored, deseeded and
    finely chopped
4 spring onions, finely sliced
1 teaspoon cumin seeds
Finely grated peel and juice of 1 lime
1 teaspoon caster sugar
15 g (^{1}/2 oz) coriander, chopped
Hash
4 tortillas
Salt and pepper

Serves 2

1. Place the refried beans in a small saucepan with the chilli sauce and gently heat through for 3 minutes.

2. In a large bowl, mix together the red peppers, spring onions, cumin seeds, lime peel and juice, sugar, coriander and hash. Season to taste with salt and pepper.

3. Lightly toast the tortillas and spread with the refried beans. Spoon over the coriander mixture, then roll up the tortillas and serve.

...careful with the weights and measures!

BUT REMEMBER...

Classic Bolognese with a Twist

Preferred hash: black
Hash quantity:
half baked = 1.5 g ($^1/16$ oz)
well baked = 1.75 g ($^1/14$ oz)

25 g (1 oz) unsalted butter
1 tablespoon olive oil
1 small onion, finely chopped
2 celery sticks, finely chopped
1 carrot, finely chopped
1 bay leaf
400 g (14 oz) lean minced beef
150 ml ($^1/4$ pint) dry white wine
Hash
150 ml ($^1/4$ pint) milk
Large pinch of freshly grated nutmeg
2 x 400 g (14 oz) tins chopped
    tomatoes
400–600 ml (14 fl oz to 1 pint) chicken
    stock
400 g (14 oz) spaghetti
Salt and black pepper
Freshly grated Parmesan cheese,
    to serve

Serves 4

I. Melt the butter with the oil in a large, heavy-based saucepan over a low heat. Add the onion, celery, carrot and bay leaf and cook for 10 minutes until softened but not coloured. Stir occasionally. Increase to a medium heat, add the minced beef and stir until the meat is no longer pink.

2. Pour in the white wine and bring to a boil. Gently simmer for 15 minutes until the liquid has evaporated, then stir in the hash, milk and nutmeg. Simmer for a further 15 minutes until the milk has evaporated. Stir in the chopped tomatoes, season and then cook, uncovered, over a very low heat for 3–5 hours. Each time the sauce begins to stick, add 100 ml ($3^1/2$ fl oz) of the stock.

3. Cook the spaghetti in a large saucepan of salted boiling water according to manufacturer's instructions. Drain, reserving a ladleful of the cooking water.

4. Return the spaghetti to the saucepan and place over a low heat. Add the sauce, stir for 30 seconds, then pour in the reserved cooking water and stir until the pasta is well coated. Serve immediately with a scattering of Parmesan.

Spinach & Cream Cheese Pizza

Preferred hash: blond
Hash quantity:
half baked = 1 g ($^1/_{28}$ oz)
well baked = 1.75 g ($^1/_{14}$ oz)

Dough
Hash
250 g (8 oz) self-raising flour
3 tablespoons olive oil
1 teaspoon salt

Topping
100 g (3$^1/_2$ oz) full-fat cream cheese
100 g (3$^1/_2$ oz) crème fraîche
2 teaspoons chopped rosemary
3 tablespoons olive oil
1 large onion, finely sliced
375 g (12 oz) baby spinach
Salt and pepper

Serves 4

1. Preheat the oven to 230°C/450°F/Gas Mark 8. Grease a large baking sheet.

2. For the pizza base, put the hash and flour in a bowl with the oil and salt. Add a scant 100 ml (3$^1/_2$ fl oz) water and mix to a soft dough, adding a little more water if the dough is too dry. Roll out the dough on a lightly floured surface into a round about 28 cm (11 inches) in diameter. Place on the prepared baking sheet and bake in the preheated oven for 3–4 minutes until a crust has formed.

3. For the topping, beat together the cream cheese, crème fraîche, rosemary and a little salt and pepper. Heat the oil in a frying pan and sauté the onion for 3–4 minutes until softened. Stir in the spinach and a little salt and pepper for about 1 minute until the spinach has just wilted.

4. Pile the spinach on to the pizza base, spreading it out until about 1 cm (¹/₂ inch) from the edge. Place spoonfuls of the cheese mixture on top of the spinach, then bake the pizza for 8 minutes or until turning golden.

Mushroom &
Couscous Sausages

Preferred hash: black
Hash quantity:
half baked = 1 g (^{1}/28 oz)
well baked = 1.75 g (^{1}/14 oz)

75 g (3 oz) couscous
3 tablespoons olive oil
1 onion, chopped
250 g (8 oz) chestnut mushrooms,
    roughly chopped
1 red chilli, deseeded and finely sliced
Hash
3 garlic cloves, roughly chopped
Small handful of mixed herbs such as
    thyme, rosemary, parsley
200 g (7 oz) whole cooked chestnuts
75 g (3 oz) fresh breadcrumbs
1 egg yolk
Oil, for pan-frying
Salt and pepper

Serves 4

1. Place the couscous in a bowl, add 6 tablespoons boiling water and let stand for 5 minutes.

2. Heat the olive oil in a frying pan, add the onion, mushrooms and chili, then fry quickly for about 5 minutes until the mushrooms are golden and the moisture has evaporated.

3. Transfer the mushroom mixture to a food processor or blender. Add the hash, garlic, herbs and chestnuts. Process until finely chopped. Turn into a large bowl and add the soaked couscous, breadcrumbs and egg yolk. Season with salt and pepper.

4. Using lightly floured hands, shape the mixture into 12 sausage shapes. Heat the oil in a frying pan and fry the sausages for about 10 minutes, turning frequently.

Kesar Cooler

Preferred hash: blond
Hash quantity:
half baked = 1 g (^{1}/28 oz)
well baked = 1.75 g (^{1}/14 oz)

1 tablespoon ground almonds
1 teaspoon saffron threads
1 tablespoon chopped pistachios,
    plus extra to decorate
^{1}/2 teaspoon crushed cardamom pods
2 tablespoons granulated sugar
Hash
900 ml (1^1/2 pints) cold milk
2–3 scoops vanilla ice cream

Serves 4

1. Put the almonds, saffron, pistachio nuts, cardamom, sugar and hash in a mortar, add 3 tablespoons hot water and, using a pestle, grind well to make a paste.

2. Transfer the paste to a food processor or blender. Add the milk and ice cream and blend until smooth.

3. Pour into chilled glasses and serve decorated with a scattering of chopped pistachios.

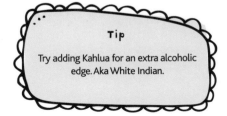

Tip

Try adding Kahlua for an extra alcoholic edge. Aka White Indian.

Chilli Cheese & Corn Cakes

Preferred hash: blond
Hash quantity:
half baked = 1 g ($^1/_{28}$ oz)
well baked = 1.75 g ($^1/_{14}$ oz)

125 g (4 oz) frozen sweetcorn, thawed
200 g (7 oz) tin butter bean, rinsed and drained
Hash
125 g (4 oz) semolina or polenta
125 g (4 oz) Cheddar cheese, shredded
$^1/_2$ teaspoon dried chilli flakes
4 tablespoons mango chutney
1 egg
Tomato or chilli sauce (optional)
Oil, for pan-frying
Salt and pepper

Serves 4

I. Place the sweetcorn and butter beans in a food processor or blender, then process until chopped into very small pieces. (Alternatively, mash with a fork in a bowl.) Transfer to a bowl, if necessary, and add the hash, semolina or polenta, cheese and chilli flakes.

2. Chop any large pieces of chutney into smaller pieces, then add the chutney and egg to the sweetcorn mixture and mix to a dough. Season with salt and pepper.

3. Using lightly floured hands, shape the mixture into 12 balls, then flatten into cakes. Heat a little oil in a frying pan, add the corn cakes, and fry gently for about 3 minutes on each side until golden. Drain on kitchen towel and serve warm with tomato or chilli sauce, if liked.

Cheesy Crumbles

Preferred hash: blond
Hash quantity:
half baked = 1 g (^{1}/28 oz)
well baked = 1.75 g (^{1}/14 oz)

125 g (4 oz) Cheddar cheese, coarsely
    shredded
4 scallions, thinly sliced
25 g (1 oz) walnuts, finely chopped
Hash
100 g (3^1/2 oz) plain flour
1 teaspoon wholegrain Dijon mustard
6 tablespoons butter

Makes 20

oh so cheesy
cheeba cheeba

I. Preheat the oven to 190°C/375°F/Gas Mark 5. Lightly grease two baking sheets. Put the cheese in a bowl. Add the spring onions and walnuts to the cheese, then stir in the hash, flour and mustard.

2. Melt the butter and add to the cheese mixture, stirring until well blended. Shape the mixture into 2.5-cm (1-inch) balls and place on the prepared baking sheets. Flatten slightly with a spatula.

3. Bake in the preheated oven for about 15 minutes until golden brown. Let cool slightly on the sheets for 2–3 minutes and then transfer to a wire rack to cool completely. These are best eaten warm or on the day they are made, but they can be stored in an airtight container in a cool place for up to three days.

Potato Drop Scones

Preferred hash: blond
Hash quantity:
half baked = 1.5 g (^{1}/16 oz)
well baked = 1.75 g (^{1}/14 oz)

500 g (1 lb 2 oz) large potatoes, peeled
    and cut into chunks
Hash
1^1/₂ teaspoons baking powder
2 eggs
75 ml (3 fl oz) full-fat milk
Salt and pepper
Oil, for pan-frying

Makes 12

1. Cook the potatoes in lightly salted boiling water for 15 minutes or until completely tender. Drain well, return to the pan and mash until smooth. Let cool slightly.

2. Beat in the hash and baking powder, then the eggs, milk and a little seasoning. Continue to beat the mixture until everything is evenly combined.

3. Heat a little oil in a heavy-based frying pan. Drop heaped spoonfuls of the mixture into the frying pan, spacing them slightly apart, and fry for 3–4 minutes until golden, turning once. Transfer to a serving plate and keep warm while frying the remainder of the potato mixture. Serve warm.

Blueberry Pancakes

Preferred hash: blond
Hash quantity:
half baked = 1.5 g (^{1}/16 oz)
well baked = 1.75 g (^{1}/14 oz)

Hash
125 g (4 oz) self-raising flour
Finely grated peel of ¹/₂ lemon
1 teaspoon baking powder
1 tablespoon caster sugar
1 egg
1 tablespoon lemon juice
150 ml (¹/₄ pint) low-fat milk
125 g (4 oz) blueberries
Maple syrup
Oil, for pan-frying
Vanilla Ice cream, to serve

Makes 10

I. Put the hash, flour, lemon peel, baking powder and sugar into a bowl. Add the egg and lemon juice, then gradually whisk in the milk until you have a smooth, thick batter. Stir in the blueberries, reserving a few for decoration.

2. Heat a frying pan or griddle, then rub it with a piece of kitchen towel drizzled with a little oil. Drop spoonfuls of the mixture, well spaced apart, on the frying pan or griddle and cook for 2–3 minutes until bubbles form on the surface and the underside is golden brown.

3. Turn the pancakes over and cook the reverse side. Wrap in a tea towel and keep hot while you cook the remainder of the mixture in the same way. Stack 3 or 4 pancakes on each plate and drizzle with maple syrup. Decorate with the reserved blueberries and serve with ice cream.

Falafel Cakes

Preferred hash: blond
Hash quantity:
half baked = 1 g (^{1}/28 oz)
well baked = 1.75 g (^{1}/14 oz)

Hash
400 g (14 oz) tin chickpeas, rinsed
     and drained
1 onion, roughly chopped
3 garlic cloves, roughly chopped
2 teaspoons cumin seeds
1 teaspoon mild chilli powder
2 tablespoons chopped mint
3 tablespoons chopped coriander
50 g (2 oz) fresh breadcrumbs
Oil, for pan-frying
Salt and pepper

Serves 4

1. Place the hash and chickpeas in a food processor or blender with the onion, garlic, spices, chopped herbs, breadcrumbs and a little salt and pepper. Process briefly to make a chunky paste.

2. Take spoonfuls of the mixture and flatten into cakes. Heat a 1-cm (^{1}/2-inch) depth of oil in a frying pan and fry half the falafel for about 3 minutes until crisp and golden, turning once. Drain on kitchen towel and keep warm while cooking the remainder.

Tip

Try dipping in hummus or taramasalata for a tasty treat. If you want to top up your THC levels, serve with the Tahini Hummus on page 66.

Oatcakes

Preferred hash: blond
Hash quantity:
half baked = 1 g (^{1}/28 oz)
well baked = 1.75 g (^{1}/14 oz)

Hash
100 g (3^1/2 oz) rolled oats
Scant ^{1}/2 cup plain flour
1 teaspoon bicarbonate soda
1 teaspoon granulated sugar
Pinch of salt
4 tablespoons butter

Makes 12

1. Preheat the oven to 180°C/350°F/Gas Mark 4. Lightly grease a baking sheet.

2. Put the hash, rolled oats, flour, bicarbonate soda, sugar and salt in a mixing bowl. Melt the butter with 1–2 tablespoons water in a small saucepan over a low heat. Pour into the oat mixture and combine to form a dough.

3. Turn the dough on to a lightly floured surface and knead it until it is no longer sticky. Add a little extra flour when kneading, if necessary.

4. Roll out the dough until 5-mm (^{1}/4-inch) thick and cut out 8-cm (3^1/4-inch) rounds with a biscuit cutter. Arrange on the prepared baking sheet and bake for 15–20 minutes or until golden. Remove to a wire rack to cool. Store in an airtight container.

oh so oaty!

Cherry Pie

Preferred hash: black
Hash quantity:
half baked = 1.5 g ($^1/16$ oz)
well baked = 1.75 g ($^1/14$ oz)

375 g (13¼ oz) sweet shortcrust pastry
250 g (8 oz) fresh or frozen cherries
    (pitted if fresh, thawed if frozen)
2 tablespoons granulated sugar
Hash
Milk, to glaze
50 g (2 oz) flaked almond, to decorate
Double cream, to serve

Serves 6

pie in the sky!

1. Preheat the oven to 190°C/375°F/Gas Mark 5. Roll out about two-thirds of the pastry on a lightly floured surface and use to line a 23-cm (9-inch) tart tin. Chill in the refrigerator for 30 minutes. Spread the cherries evenly over the pastry case and sprinkle with the sugar and hash.

2. Roll out the remaining pastry and cut into thin strips. Brush the rim of the tart with water and arrange the pastry strips in a lattice pattern over the top of the cherries. Brush the pastry with a little milk and sprinkle the pie with the flaked almond.

3. Bake in the preheated oven for 30–35 minutes or until the pastry is golden and the cherries are tender. Serve warm or cold with double cream.

Big Ideas

write your
experiences here!

Recipe	Experience	Rating
		/6
		/6
		/6
		/6
		/6
		/6

Finish the perfect munchie cake...

recipe name: _____

what a great
scooby snack!

About the Authors

A worthy supporter of the marijuana cause since high tops were in fashion, Dane Noon is an avid chef with a love of music and enjoys nothing more than taking his followers on a journey through mouth and mind. He wants to invade Guernsey.

Lex Lucid is a writer who splits his time between the jungles of Papua New Guinea and London. He enjoys witchety grubs, raucous tea parties and long haul flights, and is occasionally mistaken for someone else. He wants to bring peace to the Middle East.